C000151541

Roche Abbey

Peter Fergusson and Stuart Harrison

C000151541

CONTENTS

Tour of the Abbey

❶ BANQUETING LODGE

The Banqueting Lodge (now the ticket office), completed by 1777, was probably designed by Lancelot 'Capability' Brown, who had been hired by the 4th Earl of Scarbrough to develop the landscape. Built in the 'Gothick' style, it used stonework from the ruined abbey and medieval decorative details removed from the church, such as the pinnacles placed at the roof line, and was built for Lord Scarbrough to entertain his guests.

❷ GREAT GATEHOUSE

A Cistercian monastery consisted of a walled precinct containing a series of confined, secure enclosures, with the church and cloister at the centre of the complex. The lower parts of the precinct walls, about 3m high and some 3½ miles long, can be traced on the site's north and south sides. On the west an outer gate in this perimeter wall provided entry down a 50m long walled lane, which terminated at the great gatehouse, an imposing two-storey building set immediately below and against the limestone outcrop. Intended to impress visitors as well as to protect the security of the monastery, the present gatehouse dates from the mid 14th century and replaced an

Below: The Banqueting Lodge, now the ticket office, built in the 1770s. From here there were views of Lancelot 'Capability' Brown's Picturesque landscape

Facing page: The chapter house in the 1880s after it had been cleared. In the foreground are the remains of loose stonework from the arcade openings

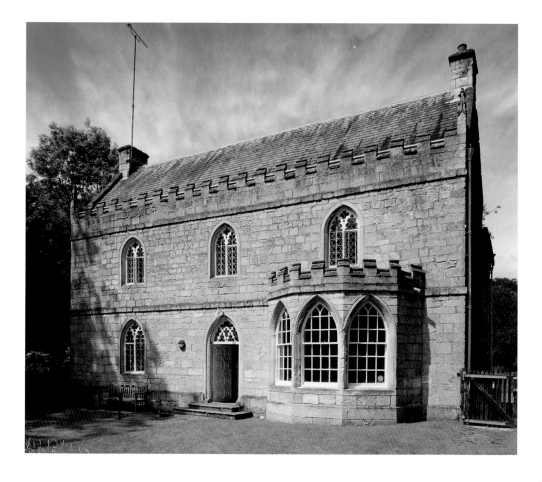

Above: The gatehouse, seen from the west with the porch and entry doorways within

Below: Close-up of a carved head of a monk on the springer capital inside the gatehouse

earlier one, of which little is known. It is one of the earliest surviving examples of a Cistercian gatehouse.

Entry to the gatehouse was through a porch, divided from an inner gate-hall by a pair of arches on which were hung two gates, the larger for carts and the smaller for pedestrians. Much of the original medieval roadway survives. An arch on the east side of the gate-hall led to the inner and outer courts.

The porch and gate-hall retain their simple chamfered rib vaults complete with carved foliate bosses (carved rib intersections) and, unusually, carved heads at the springers. The main arches are pointed and segmental to keep the vault low while still allowing sufficient headroom. Traces of painted limewash survive in places on the vaulting, and the whole building would have been similarly decorated.

Upper floor

A small doorway in the east wall opens into a stair lobby with a niche for a lamp and a circular stair to the upper floor. A single large room with benching along the outer walls occupied the space over the porch and extended to the east on a ledge of the rock face. To the south, above the gate-hall, was a smaller chamber. The large chamber was probably accessed by an external staircase to the south-east.

Monastic gatehouses were not only used to admit travellers and visitors who expected free overnight accommodation in the monastery – food was also provided daily from the porch for the destitute in the neighbourhood. The large room on the

Left: A Victorian painting of Worksop Priory gatehouse by Andrew McCallum. The gatehouse at Worksop offers a nearby parallel to Roche in date, design and sculptural ornament

Below: The gatehouse porch, where alms and food for the destitute were distributed daily

upper floor was probably used for judicial hearings, presided over by the abbot (or his delegate), who would have used the separate entry stair. Roche's landholdings generated legal matters and disputes concerning tenants and rents, access and trespass, civil order, commercial transactions and other responsibilities. The smaller rooms may have been used to store documents related to these proceedings, as well as to provide living quarters for the gatehouse keeper.

Below: Book fitting showing the Annunciation (top) and both sides of a 13th-century lead seal of Pope Innocent IV (middle and bottom), on a papal bull from Roche Abbey
Bottom: A watermill once stood in the outer court at Roche, similar perhaps to this one in the 14th-century Luttrell Psalter

❸ INNER COURT

The appearance of the area between the lodge and the church, once the monastery's inner court, is the result of the work of 'Capability' Brown who, in the 1770s, levelled off the remains of the surviving medieval buildings and covered them with soil to provide a grassed foreground from which to view the ruined church. In the medieval period the inner court contained Roche's guest house and common hall. Hospitality was a time-honoured institution for all monasteries (the word derives from the Latin *hospes*, meaning 'guest' or 'stranger'). Its importance was affirmed in Christ's words: 'I was hungry and you gave me food, I was thirsty and you gave me something to drink, I was a stranger and you welcomed me' (Matthew 25: 35). Decisions about where visitors stayed lay with the gatehouse keeper, who was a senior monk. He assigned accommodation by social rank, which he judged by how many horses and riders accompanied the visitor. Aristocracy stayed with the abbot, gentry lodged in the guest house and everyone else boarded in the common hall.

Almost certainly the remains of the guest house and common hall lie under the grass, together with related buildings such as the guest-house kitchens, washrooms, latrines, the residence and office (or checker) of the cellarer (who was, among other responsibilities, in charge of looking after guests), and the monastery's bakehouse and brewhouse.

❹ OUTER COURT

The outer court lay south of the inner court, across the Maltby Dike. It contained various buildings connected to Roche's economic life, such as the stables, mill, woolhouse, oxhouse, dovecote, tannery, fish ponds and orchards. None of these has been investigated, but documents hint at their variety and extent. After Roche was suppressed and its lands divided, a 1554 grant to William Ramsden specifies 'two orchards with little ponds'. Two of seven such 'orchards, dovecotes, fruit gardens, ponds, and other conveniences' are mentioned as lying within this area of the precinct.

CHURCH

The church was the largest and most ambitious building in every monastery. Dating from the late 1170s, or perhaps about 1180, the church at Roche was used intensively every day by the monks and lay brothers and resonated with song and communal prayer for between seven and nine hours a day, depending on the liturgical season. A Cistercian church was divided into two parts – the east part for the monks and the west part for the lay brothers – each with its own entrances, altars, stalls and furnishings. Particularly distinctive of Cistercian churches was the modest east end consisting of a short, square-ended presbytery and transepts (side arms) with square-ended, east-facing chapels. The architectural simplicity of this arrangement, contrasting with the churches of the other religious orders, reflected the simplified Cistercian liturgy. The abbot of the parent house would have checked the work on his annual visitation. Similarly, images were banned and ornament purged. Stained glass, for example, was forbidden, out of concern that it would distract the monks from their devotions. Plain glass (known as 'grisaille'), seen as a spiritual metaphor for the light of God, was used instead.

5 West front and porch

The west facade survives only as a chest-high, even-levelled wall. In the 15th century the 12th-century porch was remodelled and extended across the west front and along the west range to the lay brothers' parlour. This suggests that the porch was used during the weekly Sunday procession to bless the buildings of

Above: View of the north and south transepts with the remains of the rood screen in the foreground. This divided the monks' part of the church from that of the lay brothers
Below: A priest celebrating Mass, from a 14th-century English Cistercian manuscript

*Reconstruction of the abbey church
and cloister in about 1220*

A Abbey church

B Lay brothers' choir

C Monks' choir

D High altar

E North transept

F South transept

G Cloister

H Chapter house

I Warming room

J Refectory

K Kitchen

L Lay brothers' dormitory

the cloister, which would probably have exited through the lay brothers' parlour before returning to the church through the west doors. Some supports for the mullions of the porch's traceried windows survive.

6 Nave

Three west doorways led into a broad, high, central space, probably illuminated by a rose window, and lower flanking aisles covered with rib vaulting. Building proceeded from east to west, as indicated by changes in the bases of the piers along the nave. The five western bays were used by the lay brothers who attended services at the beginning and the end of the day. Their seating was arranged as inward-facing stalls. They entered from their dormitory via a stairway in the west bay set parallel to the aisle wall.

At the fifth bay from the west end a masonry rood-screen, about 3m high and topped by figures of the crucified Christ flanked by the Virgin Mary and St John, marked the end of the lay brothers' part of the church. The central doorway of the screen survives and is decorated with nailhead ornament, the first time this decoration appears at Roche. On either side of the doorway were two altars on a raised platform.

When the lay brothers ceased to be part of the community in the 14th century their stalls were removed. The space became a burial place for secular patrons of the abbey, and was used by local people when they attended daily offices such as

Above: The remains of the rood-screen, which divided the nave between the lay brothers and the monks
Below: The north aisle of the nave, looking east, with the transepts in the distance, showing the crossing **A** *and the screen* **B**

Above: The north side of the nave, with the remains of a chantry chapel inserted when the lay brothers ceased to be part of the community in the early 14th century

Below: Monks praying in front of an altar from a 13th-century French psalter. Each transept at Roche contained two chapels. The remains of the altar platforms are still visible in the north transept

vespers. A number of tomb slabs, some with faded inscriptions, can still be seen. On the north side, the third bay contained an elevated tomb, which was part of a chantry chapel (endowed for the singing of special Masses for the dead).

On the east side of the rood-screen is a bench where aged monks who were unable to participate in the rigours of the full cycle of services could sit. A second screen (*pulpitum*) marked the entry into the monks' choir, which occupied the two bays before the crossing. Their stalls faced inwards in two rows, one behind the other.

7 Crossing and 8 night stairs

The crossing, where the nave and transepts intersect, is defined by four large piers composed of clustered shafts that supported the low central tower. The tower housed Roche's bells, which were probably rung from the crossing. Michael Sherbrook's account of the Suppression of the abbey in 1538 (see page 33) tells us that the tower held nine bells.

A low foundation wall against the west wall of the south transept marks the position of the night stairs used by the monks when entering the church from their dormitory for the first offices or services, which took place in darkness (during daylight hours they entered through the doorway from the cloister into the next bay to the west). Before the monks turned to enter their stalls they performed a ritual laving, or washing. Although the *laver* (basin) has vanished, its position is marked by a floor drain with a quatrefoil design, at the base of the south-west crossing pier.

9 Transepts

The three-storey, rib-vaulted elevation of the transepts has an unmistakably French Gothic appearance, with pointed arches and elegant shafts. Small variations in architectural detailing suggest a sequenced building campaign, with work on the south transept a few years earlier than that on the north.

Each transept had two chapels: those on the south are more complete and retain intact rib vaults. The windows were enlarged in the 14th century with reticulated flowing tracery to admit more light and to enhance the slimmer, more complex linear design prized during the period. In the north transept the chapels retain their altar platforms as well as the arched recess for the *piscina* (the wall niche in which vessels used in the Mass were cleaned). The north wall retains the stubs of three tiers of round-headed windows and indicates a terminal wall with window ranges. This lancet arrangement with its glazed grisaille perforations brought light into the centre of the church. The central doorway in the north wall gave access to the cemetery next to the east end of the church.

Above: The south transept, showing the remains of the altar platform **A** and the outline of the piscina **B**
Left: Monks sitting in choir stalls, from an early 15th-century French psalter. The skeletons of the Pope, bishops and cardinals behind the choir stalls may be a memento mori – a reminder of the transience of life

Left: A 15th-century manuscript illustration of St Bernard and the monks of Cîteaux taking possession of the Cistercian abbey of Clairvaux, whose Gothic architecture inspired the builders of Roche Abbey
Below: A carved head found at Roche
Bottom: The pointed Gothic arch in the north chapel of the north transept

Gothic Architecture

The architecture of the church at Roche is distinctively Gothic. Invented and developed in and around Paris in the 1140s, Gothic united single structural features (such as pointed arches or rib vaults) with a different treatment of broader architectural elements such as space, massing, articulation and visual effects. Compared with the Romanesque style that had been in use since the Conquest of 1066, Gothic architecture looked lighter, displayed slimmer forms and detailing, unified spaces, and favoured larger window openings.

Gothic appeared in the north of England in the 1160s, earlier than in the south. Before its use by the Cistercians, Gothic had been employed at York Minster (c.1160s) and Lincoln Cathedral (c.1150). A three-storey elevation with rib vaults, similar to that at Roche, was used in the construction of the large Cistercian church at Kirkstead Abbey, Lincolnshire (late 1160s), and the same was employed at Newminster Abbey, Northumberland (c.1170s), the mother house of Roche. At Roche the more pronounced French character – with its precisely cut stone and elaborate decoration – derives from the use of Gothic in Cistercian abbeys in north-east France, notably Clairvaux (Aube) and Cherlieu (Franche-Comté), as well as in centres to the north-west in Picardy and Flanders.

Such links provide clues to the source from which Roche's master mason came. His presence in the north of England can probably be associated with a builder–abbot such as Richard of Clairvaux (1150–70) at Fountains, the head of the filiation to which Roche belonged. Richard had been trained at Clairvaux and was Abbot of Vauclair (Aisne) before coming to Yorkshire.

Over time the transept vaults began to spread and displace the east wall. Extensive repairs in the 1920s prevented collapse. When the church was cleared in the 1880s, traces of false black masonry lines painted on a limewashed ground were discovered. Other decoration included red painting on the vault ribs and possibly painted leaf decoration on the capitals, as at Byland Abbey, North Yorkshire.

10 Presbytery

The presbytery housed the high altar on a raised platform, the foundations of which survive against the ruined east wall. This part of the church was never enlarged, unlike at many other Cistercian monasteries in northern England, and the only changes made were enlarging the windows in the east wall in the late 14th century and inserting tracery. The capitals of the vault supports have undercut leaf decoration richer than the plain chalice capitals used in the transepts and nave. The floor has steps up to the high altar marked by changes in the internal chamfered plinth course.

The south wall retains its *piscina*, a basin for the washing of Mass vessels. To the west are the arched remains of the *sedilia* (seats for the priests officiating at the Mass), dating from the 1170s, with a later remodelling, probably of the 15th century, marked by numerous pinnacles and arched tabernacle canopies. Opposite, on the north wall, are similar traces of 15th-century tabernacle work that was part of a great tomb, possibly that of Maud, Countess of Cambridge (d.1446), a relation of the founder of the abbey (founders were usually buried on the north side of the presbytery).

Above: The gable, apex and finial of a wall tomb, possibly that of Maud, Countess of Cambridge, on the north wall of the presbytery
Below: The presbytery and north transept from the north-east

⓫ CLOISTER

The cloister formed the hub of the monastery: all the major buildings were arranged around its garth, or square, open centre. Covered alleys or walks provided access to the buildings and workspaces and opened on to the centre through arcades, parts of which were recovered through excavation. These show that the arcades consisted of twin-shafted columns on moulded bases, with waterleaf capitals, supporting elegant pointed arches. Only the foundation wall of the arcades survives.

Like the church, the cloister was divided between the monks, on the east and south sides, and the lay brothers on the west side. By custom the cloister alleys had different uses. That adjacent to the church, on the north side of the cloister, would have contained carrels (wooden desks), at which the monks read scripture or commentary for the nearly two hours of each morning devoted to the *lectio divina* ('divine reading'; see page 30). This alley was also the setting for the nightly collation, when the community assembled to hear passages from the writings of St John Cassian (360–435), an early monastic pioneer, and to receive a small drink before retiring to their dormitory.

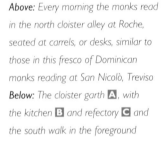

Above: Every morning the monks read in the north cloister alley at Roche, seated at carrels, or desks, similar to those in this fresco of Dominican monks reading at San Nicolò, Treviso
Below: The cloister garth **A***, with the kitchen* **B** *and refectory* **C** *and the south walk in the foreground*

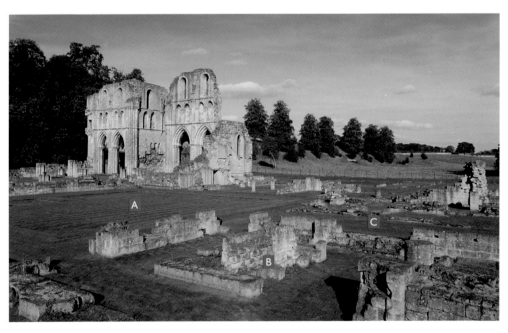

EAST RANGE

The upper storey of the east range, which contained the monks' dormitory, has entirely disappeared; what survive are the undercrofts.

🔢 Library

The first doorway on the east side of the cloister led into the library, and the room beyond it served as the sacristy (for Mass vestments and vessels). Library lists from the late 12th century suggest that a monastery the size of Roche would have held about 75 manuscripts with texts in Latin. They would have included bibles, each in several volumes with a commentary (or glosses), books by the Church Fathers (such as Saints Augustine, Ambrose and Jerome), encyclopaedias, sermons by famous Cistercian exegetes (such as St Bernard of Clairvaux and St Aelred of Rievaulx), histories, meditations and classical texts, including treatises on agriculture and medicine. Most books were kept in the cloister, near the church, for the *lectio divina*, but they were also used and stored in the church, refectory, infirmary or gardener's office. Over time the library expanded by gift, purchase or through copying (undertaken in the day room; see page 16), and in the later medieval period monks were allowed their own books. Next to the library was the *tabula*, or board, on which was chalked the daily work rota.

🔢 Chapter house and 🔢 parlour

The second doorway off the east cloister alley led to the chapter house, a rectangular room extending eastwards beyond the main range, which was the main meeting room. The monks gathered in it each morning after Mass to hear a reading from the *Rule of St Benedict*, confess faults and receive

Above: These medieval book fittings, found at Roche, would once have protected the abbey's books. Roche Abbey's library contained about 75 manuscripts in the late 12th century

Below: St Bernard and Cistercian monks gathering in the chapter house, from a 15th-century French manuscript. The monks at Roche met in the chapter house every day

Above: *The chapter house looking west, with columns dividing the space into twin aisles*
Bottom: *A length of gilded copper wire from a scourge found at Roche, similar to the one depicted in the 13th-century* Guthlac Roll *(below)*

Scourge

During the excavations of the 1880s a length of gilded copper plaited wire was found from a scourge for self-flagellation, part of the punishment regime of the abbey.

punishment, listen to commemorative *obits*, discuss secular business, receive high-ranking visitors and attend sermons on major feast days (the only time of year when they were delivered). No trace now remains of the benches on the side walls or of the burials of abbots traditionally placed in the chapter house.

The central doorway in the west wall was flanked by a pair of window arches, but little of these now remain. Two piers supported vaults, as did a third pier, which has now been removed. On the exterior there are buttresses and deeply moulded plinths. Photographs of the 1880s clearances show considerable architectural debris surviving from the chapter house vault, including advanced three-rib and five-rib vault designs (rather than the simpler four-rib pattern), which indicates that the original vault was altered or replaced, perhaps reflecting an increase in the size of the community. The evidence also shows that the eastern bay vault was set at a higher level, which meant that the windows could have been taller and brought more light into the space. At the Suppression it seems that the chapter house was stripped of its furnishings. The 1880s photographs indicate that some walls, including those in the chapter house, were refaced in the 1920s, and this has caused confusion over the interpretation of the ruins.

To the south of the chapter house was the parlour, where monks could speak to one another for a brief period each day. Traces of a doorway at each end indicate that it also functioned as a passageway to the infirmary.

🔢 Day room and 🔢 latrine

The rooms beyond the parlour served as the day rooms for Roche's novices and monks. The monks' room was used for the copying of manuscripts or carrying on of trades, such as book production or metalworking. Both rooms were vaulted from a central row of piers. Sockets in the piers show evidence for timber partitions that were probably a later alteration. A doorway midway down the east wall gave access to the latrines, a two-storey building over the dike with the upper floor (accessed from the dormitory for night-time use) containing seats separated by low screens set against the south wall. Doorways at the south end of the day room led to the abbot's house complex and on the west side to an unusual square room, whose purpose is unknown. A second extension 100 years later, perhaps a misericord (a room for the eating of meat), included a large fireplace built of tiles. The eating of meat was forbidden in the Rule of St Benedict but the Pope sanctioned misericords in the 1340s, so that meat could be eaten but in a separate space.

17 Infirmary

Three infirmaries were provided in the monastery – for monks, lay brothers (see page 22) and guests. The monks' infirmary was traditionally located parallel to the east range but was connected to it by a covered alley. Hence the sick and aged monks were separated from the daily life around the cloister, but were not isolated. At Roche such an alley led from the novices' day room and ended at a doorway, perhaps part of the infirmary hall. The lay brothers' infirmary was aisled and so it can be assumed that the monks' infirmary probably was too. The infirmary had its own chapel, bath-house, latrines, kitchen (the Rule of St Benedict permitted meat for the sick) and infirmarer's office, together with his medicinal herb garden. These buildings probably lay immediately to the south-east.

Above: A sick monk in bed being tended by another monk, who is examining a urine sample, from an English 15th-century manuscript. There were three separate infirmaries at Roche
Below: The day room at Roche, which was once vaulted

Above: Two monks, forming the letter 'M', are shown folding a length of linen in a 12th-century French manuscript. The monks at Roche Abbey dried their wet habits in the warming room

Below: Christ washing the feet of the disciples from a 13th-century French manuscript. The abbot of Roche washed the monks' feet every week in the laver, or wash basin

Bottom: The remains of the laver in the south aisle of the cloister

SOUTH RANGE

18 Day stairs

From the east, the first two doorways on the south side of the cloister open to the day stairs and to the warming room. The former corresponds to important changes made to the south range in the early 1170s (see page 29). The day stairs, of which the first treads remain, led to the monks' dormitory and included a small 'understairs' room that has holes at regular intervals indicating the insertion of panelling in the later medieval period. The presence of panelling suggests that this must have been an important room, perhaps the abbot's study.

19 Warming room

In this room the monks would warm themselves after the offices in the unheated church, have their heads shaved for the tonsure and undergo bleeding (deemed an aid to health and a curb to sexual appetite, and followed by several days' recuperation in the infirmary). The remains of two fireplaces survive. The firebacks are made of roof tiles probably reused from earlier buildings which had subsequently been reroofed with lead. The room also contained a tub for washing woollen habits, which were dried on lines in the cloister arcades in fair weather or in the warming room in wet weather.

20 *Laver*

Next to the refectory doorway are the remains of the monks' *laver*, in which they would have washed their hands before their meal in the refectory. Pipes channelled spring water to fill the shallow basin running the length of the wall. The *laver* was also used during the late afternoon on Saturdays, when the abbot washed the feet of the monks, a ritual that re-enacted Christ's washing of the feet of the disciples and his command to love one another. The *laver* had an arcaded design but only one moulded base remains at the west end. Each trough retains traces of chases for the lead pipes and taps, and also the drains.

21 Refectory

The refectory was a well-lit, spacious room projecting at right angles to the south cloister alley. The refectory, like the monks' day room, spans the Maltby Dike, an arrangement also found at Fountains Abbey, where the buildings bridge the river Skell.

The monks entered and left the refectory in procession. They sat on stone benching at wooden-topped and cloth-covered tables on stone legs, one of which can be seen on the east side, projecting through the grass. The abbot and senior office holders were seated at a dais at the south end. The walls were whitewashed and painted, probably with false jointing to resemble masonry, and the room was provided generously with glazed windows.

Only a single cooked meal was provided, served in the late morning. Meals were strictly vegetarian as the *Rule of St Benedict* forbids the eating of the flesh of four-footed animals. Potage, a thick soup served with bread and two vegetables (with beans and leeks as staples), was served on wooden dishes. On special feast days, eggs and fish were allowed, together with small amounts, or pittances, of delicacies such as figs or raisins, and fruit in season. Beer (brewed without hops) was the main drink. Conversation at meals was prohibited and the monks listened to one of their number reading, mostly from the Bible. The reader stood at an elevated lectern, and the lobby of the staircase serving it survives against the west wall over the dike.

22 Kitchen

The kitchen supplied food to the monks' and lay brothers' refectories which flanked it on either side. Dishes were dispensed through hatches in the east and west walls respectively. In the central area are the great hearths for cooking. The large central flue stack would have been surrounded by a series of rib vaults – the stone roof reducing the risk of fire. In the south wall an open arch provided ventilation, and wood was brought in through it to fuel the fires.

Above: Detail of Benedictine monks dining in a refectory, from a 15th-century French manuscript. The monks at Roche also sat at cloth-covered tables with the abbot and senior monks raised slightly on a dais

Below: View of the south range showing, from the left, the warming house **A***, the refectory* **B***, the kitchen* **C** *and the kitchen hearths* **D**

Below: A monk and a lay brother felling a tree, from a 12th-century French Cistercian manuscript. The lay brothers worked on Roche's farms and originally outnumbered the monks by nearly two to one

WEST RANGE

The west range housed Roche's lay brothers. When it was built in about 1180 there would have been about 100 lay brothers. Only about one-third of them, however, would have worked on farms within walking distance of the monastery. The other two-thirds worked 30 or more miles away, and lived on the granges (outlying farms), returning to the monastery only for the major feast days. This explains why the west range was smaller than the east range, even though the lay brothers originally outnumbered the monks nearly two to one. From about 1300, when the lay brothers had disappeared from the monastery, to the Suppression in 1538 much of the west range was remodelled, as happened at other Cistercian monasteries in Yorkshire such as Rievaulx. The southern part of the range was adapted for additional guest accommodation, to meet the demand made by visitors in need of overnight stays and a meal beyond what was provided in the adjacent guest houses.

23 Night stairs and 24 store room

The lay brothers' range, like that of the monks, had a parlour and refectory on the ground floor and a dormitory above. The entire upper storey has disappeared. Only the lower courses of the undercroft survive. The pier bases supporting the lay brothers' night stairs survive where the range joined the west end of the church; this stair allowed them access from their dormitory to the church for the early morning office before they left for their manual daytime work. The room next to the church probably served as the cellar to store food and supplies. A door into the cloister at the northern end was blocked in about 1200, possibly in order to reduce the level of contact between monks and lay brothers, which marked the development of a formal separation between the lay brothers and monks.

25 Lay brothers' parlour and 26 refectory

A passage in the middle of the ground floor connected to the cloister and served as a parlour where the lay brothers might meet relatives. Extending southwards from the passage was a fine, vaulted room, six bays in length, which formed the lay brothers' refectory. The food hatch to the kitchen is marked by a foot recess at the base of the wall. Traces of two large windows remain in the south wall. Both the west and south walls have arches at their bases for the latrine drain that runs underneath the room.

In the north-west corner a doorway gives access to a small room, most probably the office of the cellarer who had charge of the abbey's supplies and those of the guest houses in the inner court to the west. The west wall of this building was extended northwards to form a narrow porch to the church (see page 7).

Water Channels

Water was critical to all monasteries for health and hygiene, and as a source of power for the mills. The Maltby Dike, the monastery's main water source, canalized by the monks in the 12th century, bisects the site from west to east. A second water channel was created from the Hooton Dike, running south to north. It joins the Maltby Dike at the two-storey monks' latrine building. Spring water for drinking and washing would have been piped in a conduit to supply the *lavers*, kitchens, infirmary and guest houses. The pipe runs have not been traced, and the lead pipework would have been taken up for scrap at the Suppression.

In the main channel two cutwaters survive: one to the west of the lodge and the other at the east end of the site partly under the public pathway leading to Laughton Pond. A building over the latter is shown in Samuel Buck's engraving of 1725 (see page 35), but this was most probably a post-Suppression reuse of a monastic building. It was demolished in the 1770s by 'Capability' Brown as part of his construction of a meandering stream to replace the directed channels and his creation of a lake over the south part of the monastic precinct.

In the early 1930s the main channels were rediscovered in the clearances undertaken by the Office of Works. They were dug out and restored to use. While much remains to be investigated about the water system at Roche, the channels bring back the sound of the cleansing waters that would have been familiar to the medieval monastic community and its visitors.

Above: The Maltby Dike water channel, looking west. Water was used to power the abbey's mill, as well as for domestic use
Left: Detail of the water and drainage system at Canterbury Cathedral, c.1160, showing the fish pond (upper left) and the laving fountains (centre and top)

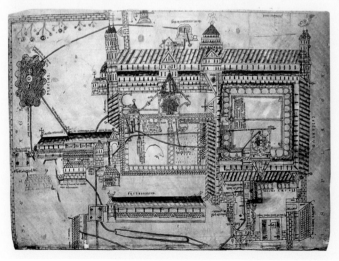

Above: The lay brothers' infirmary, on the south bank of the Maltby Dike. The infirmary was an aisled hall with beds arranged in the side aisles

Below: A replica of the seal of Roche Abbey, showing a 13th-century abbot and the inscription: SIGILLUM ABBATIS DE RUPE (seal of the abbot of Roche)

OUTSIDE THE CLOISTER
27 Lay brothers' infirmary
The lay brothers' infirmary was on the south bank of the beck. It was connected to the inner court by a bridge, traces of which remain in the water channel. A separate kitchen and infirmarer's residence would have been nearby. The interior of the lay brothers' infirmary took the form of a hall, much like a church with a wide, high central space and narrow lower aisles, which contained the beds. There were probably three beds per bay for a total of 18 patients. A fireplace in the east wall provided heat. Chests for bedding and blankets and tables for record-keeping stood in the centre of the room. An unexcavated area to the west probably retains the foundations for a kitchen serving the patients.

Like the west range, the lay brothers' infirmary was also changed following their departure from the community (see page 31). The aisle walls were renewed, and an additional space in the south-west corner screened off and heated. The building served thereafter as an additional guest house.

28 Abbot's house
East of the lay brothers' infirmary lies a complex of buildings, the purpose of which has never been resolved. They mirror those in the south range of the cloister and include a bakehouse and a kitchen, and two chamber blocks around a cloister court. At least one of these blocks must be the abbot's house, probably the easternmost, which dates from the early

13th century. Abbots were obliged to provide aristocratic guests with hospitality, and this explains the building's size and the provision of an interior court. Related structures to the east remain as humps disappearing into the adjacent wood beyond the public footpath and the one leading to the Laughton Pond.

The north end of the abbot's two-storeyed house connected to the monks' latrine, and therefore provided access to their dormitory in accordance with Cistercian legislation requiring that the abbot sleep in the same place as his brethren. The east wall has a generous window range and a hearth at the south end. Remodellings of this building show that it was periodically updated but the sequence of changes is difficult to identify.

29 Abbot's hall

Parallel to the south walk of the interior court is a further substantial building from the 14th century. Its purpose remains a puzzle. Probably added to increase accommodation in the adjacent abbot's house, it was constructed originally as a large single-storey hall with side benches and a central hearth. A later remodelling in the 1400s divided the space into three separate rooms with a window-lit latrine projecting over the Hooton Dike on the south, and the east end was converted to a two-storey apartment. Further buildings evidently extended to the south and south-east.

Below: The remains of the kitchen block serving the abbot's house, which would once have been an imposing building used to accommodate important guests

History of the Abbey

THE EARLY ABBEY

Roche's foundation followed the procedures ordained by the Cistercian order, which specified which buildings should be raised before a new foundation party moved to a site, in order to avoid the wrong choice of location. The founding charter, dated 30 August 1147, lists two local lords, Richard de Bully, Lord of Maltby, and Richard, son of Turgis, as the donors of the land in the 3km-long valley. Their lands lay on either side of the Maltby Dike, which divided the valley, and, since it was unclear on which side the monks would choose to build, the charter specified that credit for the new monastery should be shared by both founders.

The narrow valley and the dominating rock outcrops recalled the site, 45 miles to the north, of Fountains Abbey, one of the principal Cistercian monasteries in England and the success of which the new community hoped to emulate. Since all Cistercian monasteries were dedicated to the Virgin Mary, their names derived from a distinctive local feature. Roche was thus named Sancta Maria de Rupe (from the Latin *rupes*, meaning 'rock' or 'cliff') after the rock outcrops.

The first community at Roche in 1147 was a colony or daughter house from another Cistercian abbey, Newminster in Northumberland. The founding party consisted of 12 monks and an abbot (a group modelled on biblical accounts of the apostles' common life together) and about 20 lay brothers.

Above: A 15th-century lead pilgrim badge of St Margaret of Antioch, found at Roche Abbey
Below: Roche Abbey lies in a secluded valley, surrounded by rock outcrops

Facing page: Roche Abbey from across the weir on Maltby Dike, photographed by the celebrated architectural photographer John Gay in the 1950s

The Cistercians

Widespread admiration of the order's spiritual discipline and simplicity of life led benefactors to offer gifts of land, money and protection

In western Europe groups of men began living together under the discipline of a written 'rule' derived from the monastic tradition established by St Benedict of Nursia (d.547) at the hilltop monastery of Monte Cassino in Italy, about 80 miles south of Rome. Over the following centuries calls from within the community constantly arose for a more rigorous adherence to the Rule of St Benedict. The Rule set out a wide range of prescriptions for religious foundations, covering – in more than 70 chapters – everything from diet and church services to the treatment of guests and the working day. One such reform movement was the Cistercian order, which originated in 1098 at Cîteaux in Burgundy. They were known as the white monks owing to the colour of their habits (as opposed to the black of other monastic orders). The order began to expand between 1110 and 1120, and its subsequent growth was without parallel in monastic history. By 1200 more than 600 Cistercian monasteries had been established across Europe and the eastern Mediterranean.

The first Cistercian monastery in England was at Waverley, Surrey, established in 1128. Cistercian monks came to the North in 1132, when Rievaulx in the North York Moors was founded as the planned headquarters for the spiritual renewal of the region. By the end of King Stephen's reign in 1154 the Cistercian order had established 46 monasteries in England out of an eventual total of 64. These, plus all those of other religious orders in England, were suppressed between 1536 and 1539.

The success of the Cistercians derived from a new conception of the cloistered community, fashioned around a simpler and more austere disciplined life directed to the worship of God and fraternal fellowship. An insistence on poverty required that each monastery be self-sufficient. To make this model plausible economically, the monks offered vocations to lay brothers whose main responsibility consisted of demanding manual agricultural work. In general, lay brothers had little education and came

Above: A monk harvesting corn, from a 12th-century French manuscript. Roche Abbey was self-sufficient and grew its own crops

Left: Rievaulx Abbey, the first Cistercian abbey in Yorkshire

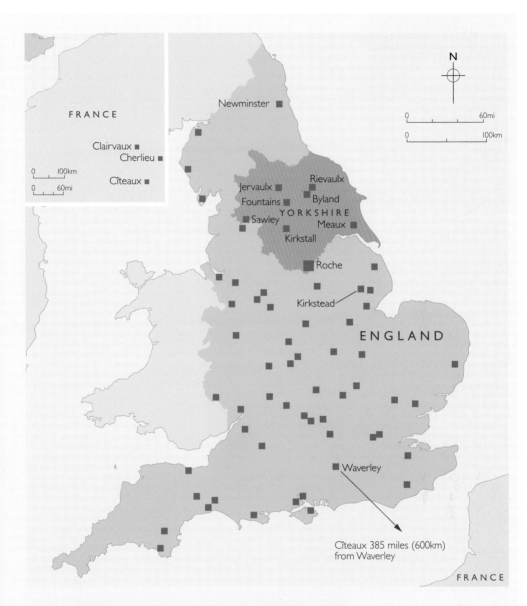

N

FRANCE

Clairvaux ■
Cherlieu ■
Cîteaux ■

0   100km
0   60mi

0   60mi
0   100km

Newminster ■

Jervaulx ■   Rievaulx ■
Fountains ■   Byland ■
■ Sawley   YORKSHIRE
■ Kirkstall   Meaux ■

■ Roche

Kirkstead

ENGLAND

■ Waverley

Cîteaux 385 miles (600km)
from Waverley

FRANCE

from modest backgrounds, and so had previously been excluded from monastic life. In Cistercian monasteries the lay brothers shared the church and cloister with the monks, a strikingly original idea at the time and one which held great appeal. While the monks wore white habits and were clean-shaven, the lay brothers wore brown habits and were bearded. Like the monks, however, the lay brothers took vows of poverty, chastity, and obedience.

Widespread admiration of the order's spiritual discipline and simplicity of life led benefactors to offer gifts of land, money and protection. In return they received prayer and friendship, benefited from the monasteries' agricultural and cattle-raising skills, drew on the knowledge of hydraulics honed from land clearances, and capitalized on the international contacts and hospitality resulting from the order's network across Europe.

Above: Map of the Cistercian houses in England, showing their distribution across the country. Within 26 years of the first mission to England in 1128, 46 Cistercian monasteries had been founded

Above: A set of folding scales and two
coin weights, found at Roche Abbey.
They would have been used for
weighing precious items such as coins,
jewels, medicine or spices
Below: King Louis VI watching a
church being built, from the
14th-century Grandes Chroniques
de France. The abbey church at
Roche was built in the late 1170s,
or perhaps as late as 1180

THE ABBEY IN ITS HEYDAY

Settled initially in timber buildings (probably in the area of
the cloister), the Roche community began to prosper as a
self-sufficient economic entity. Three early abbots – Dionysus
(1159–71), Hugh de Wadsworth (1179–84) and Osmund
(1184–c.1213) – negotiated additional grants of land for
granges and upland grazing for sheep and horse breeding in
south Yorkshire, Lincolnshire and Nottinghamshire. This
expansion generated income that enabled the construction of
permanent stone buildings to replace the early wooden ones.

The uniformity and precision in the cutting of the limestone
blocks used for construction at Roche is notable. The fine-
quality masonry was distinctively French, especially in terms
of the cutting of the stone ashlars. Later visitors such as the
Earl of Surrey in 1345 hailed the abbey's stonework as
magnificentiam ('magnificent') and even the Suppression
commissioners 200 years later referred to the abbey as being
'a very fair-built house all of freestone'. The contrast with
the rough and often untidy stonework used by the Cistercians
in their earlier monasteries is striking.

In the 1170s Roche's founders donated large quantities of
timber 'for the completion' of the buildings, probably for the
roofs. A general confirmation of the abbey's lands, possessions,
rights and privileges by Pope Urban III (1185–7) in 1186 may
well have marked the completion of the main building
campaigns. Subsequent papal confirmations in 1238 and 1241
probably followed the conclusion of smaller-scale undertakings.
That of 1241 specified an endowment for the dedication of
the church following the death of Idonea de Vipont, the heiress
of one of the co-founders, who gave Roche the manor of
Sandbeck and was buried in the abbey church, possibly on the
north side of the presbytery.

In the early 1170s an important re-ordering of the south claustral range took place at Roche and at all Cistercian monasteries. The day stairs were moved from the east range to the south range, and the refectory was positioned at 90 degrees (north–south) to the south alley instead of parallel to it (east–west). The warming room was placed on the east side of the refectory and the kitchen on the west. The new arrangement could accommodate increased numbers (simply by extending the length of the refectory), but also made it possible for monks to serve as cooks without leaving the cloister – part of the stricter Cistercian discipline – as they did in the monasteries of other orders where kitchens lay outside the cloister to protect against the spread of fire.

At its peak, about 1175, the monastery numbered about 50 monks and 100 working lay brothers and servants. It was thus medium-sized compared with the Cistercian order's seven other Yorkshire monasteries, including Rievaulx (with more than 600 men) and Fountains (with 350 men).

Reconstruction of Roche Abbey in its heyday in about 1450

A *Abbey church*
B *Cloister*
C *Lay brothers' refectory with dormitory above*
D *Lay brothers' infirmary*
E *Refectory*
F *Dormitory*
G *Latrine*
H *Abbot's cloister*
I *Abbot's house*
J *Abbot's hall*
K *Infirmary hall*
L *Infirmary kitchen*
M *Gatehouse*

The Daily Life of Monks at Roche

Work of God (*opus dei*)

The monks' daily schedule (*horarium*) was divided into three distinct parts. The most important was the cycle of seven separate offices (or services) directed to the praise of God (the *opus dei*). They began with Matins at 2.30am and were based on the example of the Hebrew psalmist who praised God seven times a day and rose at midnight to give thanks (Psalm 119). To these the monks added the daily celebration of Mass, a commemoration of Christ's death and an affirmation of a life of fraternal devotion.

Divine reading (*lectio divina*)

The second part of the daily routine was the *lectio divina* ('divine reading'). Monks had some education and could read Latin and about one-third were also ordained priests with the proportion steadily rising during the later medieval period. Reading was based on the Bible or Church Fathers and lasted about two hours.

Manual work (*opus manuum*)

The third part of the monks' day involved manual labour (the *opus manuum*). This lasted between two and four hours depending on the time of year and the weather and included such activities as gardening, manuscript copying and cleaning. Both the *opus dei* and the *lectio divina* took place within the confines of the

cloister and it was there that most of the life of the monks was passed.

Lay brothers

The lay brothers, in contrast, took part in only two daily services, in the early morning and evening. After the morning service they left the monastery to undertake work on nearby farms. Those working at some distance on the granges or sheep pastures lived there and returned to the monastery only for important religious festivals.

Above: Illuminated letter from a copy of the Cistercian Rule, which set out the schedule of the monks' day

Below: A medieval copper thimble, found at Roche

THE DECLINE OF THE LAY BROTHERS

Over time the egalitarian impulse of the early Cistercians gave way to a more segregated class structure, with a more apparent hierarchy within the community. Towards the mid 13th century competition to recruit both monks and lay brothers came from the new urban mendicant movements, notably the Franciscans and Dominicans.

The decline of the lay brothers as a component of Cistercian life was greatly hastened by the outbreak of the great murrain (sheep scab) in the mid 1270s. This disease decimated flocks and imperilled the economies of many Cistercian monasteries which depended on wool. The size of Roche's flock is unknown. By comparison with the known figures for the other Cistercian abbeys in Yorkshire, however, an estimate of about 5,000 sheep before the murrain seems plausible.

Fewer lay brothers meant that monastic lands were leased out to tenants in return for rental income. The buildings they had once used now lay empty and were modified to serve new purposes.

A chronicle detailing the early history of the monastery was probably composed, as at other monasteries, but it has not survived. Charters carry scattered mentions of the monks and abbots as witnesses, and other documents record their roles in regional affairs, some concerning matters such as trespass or damage to property on the granges or in the forests. In 1361, there were complaints against monks for carrying arms and failing to pay salaries. Such involvement with secular society – and friction with neighbours – was a standard consequence of any religious institution owning lands and manors.

Greater difficulty followed Scottish incursions into Yorkshire after the defeat of the English at the battle of Bannockburn in 1314. More devastating still, the Black Death in the late 1340s killed several monks. A document records that by 1380 the Roche community numbered 15 monks and only a single lay brother. The last 150 years of Roche's history appear relatively uneventful.

Above: Monks chopping wood, from a 12th-century French manuscript. The proportion of lay brothers to monks dropped from a peak of about 70 per cent at the start of the 13th century to 10 per cent by the end of the 13th century

Below: Burying victims of the Black Death at Tournai, 1349. Several monks at Roche lost their lives to the Black Death in the late 1340s

THE SUPPRESSION AND AFTER

In the late 1530s, England's monasteries were suppressed by Henry VIII (r.1509–47) and his chief minister Thomas Cromwell, and their wealth and assets were seized by the Crown. Roche was suppressed on 23 June 1538 by the commissioners of the king in a brief ceremony in the chapter house. The commissioners included two notorious canon lawyers, Doctors Richard Layton and Thomas Legh, who were renowned for their bullying tactics and rigorous questioning. A visit two years earlier had seen them compile a list of assets, solicit information about sexual misconduct and condemn superstitions such as the veneration by local people of a crucifix in a natural rock formation within the precinct. Well aware of suppressions at other monasteries, the Roche monks and novices knew that acquiescence to the Suppression led to modest pensions, whereas opposition would be branded as treason, followed by forcible ejection, arrest and death by hanging unless recantation was forthcoming. They signed the Deed of Surrender and handed over the keys to the buildings.

At this time the community consisted of 17 monks and 4 novices, and an unknown number of paid servants. The monks each probably received subsistence pensions of £5 a year, and each of the novices half that amount. Twenty shillings was provided to everyone towards new clothing. The servants each received half a year's wages. Roche's last abbot, Henry Cundal, fared better: he received an annual pension of £33, was allowed to keep his books and a quarter of the abbey's plate, and was provided with 'cattle and household stuff'. He lived for another 16 years at Tickhill, not far from Roche

Above: Iron keys, found at Roche, dating from the time of the abbey
Below: The Deed of Surrender, signed at Roche Abbey on 23 June 1538

'All Things of Price Were Spoiled'

The suppression of Roche was recorded by Michael Sherbrook (1535–1610), a rector of the nearby parish of Wickersley. His account ranks as one of the most important sources detailing a monastery's destruction. The events he describes at Roche took place when he was a child and were related to him by his father and uncle.

Sherbrook recalled the respect for the life and practice of religion at Roche right up to the time of the Suppression. People from nearby villages attended vespers in the abbey church, for example, but he was surprised at the speed with which these attitudes changed when the opportunity arose to pillage the monastery.

Between the king's commissioners' visit in 1536 and the Suppression in 1538, Sherbrook reported that the monks offered visitors a range of items for sale, including the doors to their cells.

Having inventoried all the monastery's possessions following its official surrender, the commissioners arranged for the disposal of some items through public auction. Floor tiles were pulled up, window glass dismantled and tombs defaced. Such work took time and Sherbrook noted that even a year later he recalled seeing eight or nine bells hanging in the church tower. He also reported that his father had bought several loads of timber from the steeple.

Before any movable items could be sold, however, a local mob descended on the monastery and stole what it could. Similar incidents occurred at other suppressed monasteries.

'It would have pitied any heart,' Sherbrook's father told his son, 'to see the tearing up of the lead, the plucking up of boards and throwing down of the rafters … All things of price were either spoiled, carped [plucked] away or defaced to the uttermost … and it seemed that every person bent himself to filch and spoil what he could.'

The abbey's manuscripts, such as service books, were torn apart and the parchment was used to mend the tarpaulins of carts. After ransacking the church, the mob turned its attention to all the other buildings. The only things spared were '… the ox-houses and swinecoates and such other houses of office that stood without the walls'. These remained intact along with the mill, as they were respected and considered useful to the economy of the local area.

Above: *Rioters pillage a house in Paris, from a 14th-century manuscript. The church at Roche was ransacked in 1538 and valuable items were stolen*

Right: Bishop Robert Sherburne with
Henry VIII, who suppressed the
monasteries in the 1530s. The king's
agents stripped Roche's roofs of lead
and removed other valuables
Below: Engraving of Roche Abbey by
the Buck brothers in 1725. By this
time, the abbey church had lost its
roof and trees were growing among
the ruins

Abbey, where he served a small parish as priest. Roche's other
office holders, such as the cellarer and sacrist, as well as some
of the monks, also eked out their pensions by working as
priests in the neighbourhood. Happily, records, such as wills,
show that a connection continued among them.

Immediately after the surrender the commissioners made
an exhaustive inventory of all the monastery's possessions,
ranging from liturgical objects to doors, windows, glass,
furniture and other movable items. The inventory listing of 80
oxen, 5 carthorses, 120 sheep and 40 pigs provides a picture

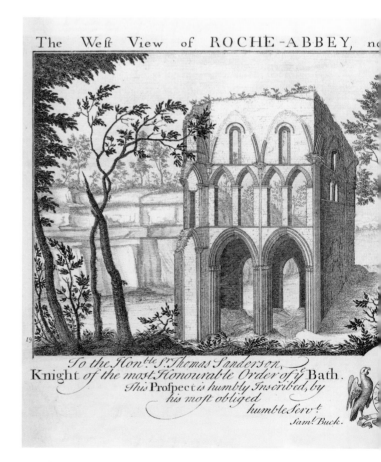

The West View of ROCHE-ABBEY, ne

To the Honble Sr Thomas Sanderson,
Knight of the most Honourable Order of y^e Bath.
This Prospect is humbly Inscribed, by
his most obliged
humble Servt
Saml Buck.

of the monastery's continuing prosperity. The king's agents
were made to strip the roofs of lead, which was melted down
using the monks' wooden choir stalls as fuel for the fire pits.

After the Suppression, ownership of the valley and its
adjacent lands passed through a succession of private hands. By
1627 it was in the possession of Robert Saunderson of
Fillingham in Lincolnshire, whose son was created Viscount
Castleton in the peerage of Ireland. When his descendants
died out in the early 18th century, the estates were left to a
cousin, Thomas Lumley (c.1691–1752), who became 3rd Earl
of Scarbrough. His heirs remain the landowners, although the
monastery remains fall under the care of English Heritage.

A re-evaluation of the site in the early 18th century was
sparked by a rising awareness of England's antiquities,
manifested in the formation of learned groups such as the
Society of Antiquaries of London in 1707. Among other
initiatives, the society sponsored in 1726 a project to illustrate
England's castles and abbeys. The published engraving of Roche
by the Buck Brothers (see below) shows the east end of the
church roofless, and rib vaults lying in heaps with trees rooted
among them. The one small building shown in the distance to
the right of the transepts was probably a post-Suppression
structure (see page 21). The abbey's medieval watercourse,
however, remained intact.

Tickhill in YORK-SHIRE. — 1728.

This Abbey was founded in the year 1147, by Rich.
de Builli, & Richard Fitz Turgis, & was of the
Cistercian Order, & belongs now, to the Honourable
S.ʳ Tho: Saunderson.

J. Buck delin. et sculp.ᵗ

Above: Portrait of Lancelot 'Capability' Brown by Richard Cosway, c.1770–5. Brown was hired by Lord Scarbrough in 1774 to landscape the ruins of the abbey

Below: *A distant view of Roche Abbey by Francis Chesham, after Paul Sandby, 1779, showing the abbey in a Picturesque setting*

THE CREATION OF A PICTURESQUE SETTING

In the late 18th century literary fashion reappraised the site, prizing its overgrown and disordered condition as a representation of unmediated nature. In addition, the shattered monastic buildings evoked the nation's past. In 1772 Horace Walpole praised Roche's owner, the 4th Earl of Scarbrough (1725–82), for leaving the site as a ruin, surmising that 'he [the earl] was afraid of ghosts' and characterizing the monastic remains as lying hidden in a 'venerable chasm' (as he described the valley). To enhance these qualities so admired at the time Lord Scarbrough hired, in 1774, the celebrated landscape gardener Lancelot 'Capability' Brown (1716–83) to reconstruct the entire valley so that it would, in the words of the surviving contract, 'accord with Poet's Feeling and Painter's Eye'.

To achieve this 'pictured' (Picturesque) effect, Brown devised ambitious and hugely expensive works. He planted asymmetrical tree groups, exposed the rock outcrops, engineered Laughton Pond to form a cascade, turned the medieval water channel into a meandering stream and created an ornamental lake over the monastery's southern buildings, complete with four irregular islands. He also levelled off the remains of the west parts of the church and inner court and covered them with grass to create a verdant foreground to the Picturesque tableau seen from the Banqueting Lodge, built for Lord Scarbrough to entertain his guests. Similar buildings were constructed by the later aristocratic owners of Fountains (the Banqueting House, 1774) and Rievaulx (the Temples, 1770s).

Taken by carriage the 1½ miles from the earl's country house of Sandbeck Park, the guests combined dining with philosophical conversation about the role of art in landscape

theory. Prompted by Brown's newly constructed tableau, conversation was expected to equate 'nature' with 'freedom', and to draw pointed contrasts between Roche's liberated nature, featuring idealized (though neatened) historical ruins, and the regularized geometry imposed on French landscapes, which epitomized royal domination. Such discussions should be seen in the context of contemporary Enlightenment philosophy and political revolution in France and America.

Today 'Capability' Brown's Picturesque landscape is still recognizable outside the fenced abbey precinct: in the Laughton Pond and waterfall, the exposed irregular rocky outcrops, and the studied contrast of pastoral meadow and dense woods on the east and south sides of the site.

Above: Watercolour of Roche Abbey by Paul Sandby, c.1770s, showing the abbey ruins in an idealized, Romantic landscape

Parties at Roche

The Banqueting Lodge was designed for entertaining and for viewing the landscape. In 1777, the Earl of Scarbrough's eldest son, Viscount Lumley, held a party here. It must have been quite a celebration, as there is a record in the Sandbeck Park archives for a payment for the post-party clean-up.

Above left: The Banqueting Lodge, built for Lord Scarbrough in the 18th century for entertaining
Above: Sandbeck Park, seat of Lord Scarbrough, by Alexander Francis Lydon, c.1880

Above: The 9th Earl of Scarbrough, who instigated a series of clearances of the site in the mid 19th century

Below: Excavating the cloister in 1885. On the left is the 10th Earl of Scarbrough; the scholar William St John Hope stands next to him, holding a pickaxe; and the Reverend William Travis Travis is on the right

ANTIQUARIAN INVESTIGATIONS

Brown's work at Roche was his first attempt to enhance an historic ruin and not all contemporary critics applauded it. William Gilpin conceded that the lake formed 'a very beautiful scene' but feared that it was 'too magnificent and too artificial an appendage to be in union with the ruins of an abbey'. More rigorous dissent followed nearly a century later. In the 1850s James Aveling, a local antiquarian who conducted the first clearances, referred to 'the havoc created by Brown' (according to the landscape critic, Fairbank, writing in 1894); and others accused Brown of 'being let loose on the place … covering up foundations and pulling down walls'. A new generation of landowners, who wanted the past to be scientifically revealed and to be 'verified' by the newly invented medium of photography, cared little about a generic Picturesque ruin. This required undoing Brown's work.

This laborious process would take the best part of 80 years to complete. It began in the late 1850s when Aveling, with the permission of the 9th Earl of Scarbrough (1813–84), began a decade-long series of small-scale excavations. His goal was to determine the ground plan of the church and cloister, about which nothing was then known. His pioneering publication on Roche of 1870, the first monograph on any monastic site in Britain, exemplifies this new attitude towards the past.

Larger-scale clearance followed in the mid 1880s, much of it led in person by the 10th Earl of Scarbrough with the help of his nephews. The earl's brother-in-law, William Orde-Powlett, recorded the process through photography.

This family enterprise, supported by estate workmen, emptied the medieval buildings of hundreds of tons of wreckage left after the Suppression and Brown's landscaping and infilling of the spaces between the broken walls. It was notably helped by two important scholars, J T Micklethwaite and William St John Hope. Micklethwaite, an architect, later became Surveyor of Westminster Abbey, and Hope, at the time master at Repton School in Derbyshire, was appointed Assistant Secretary of the Society of Antiquaries of London in 1885 and became England's foremost authority on medieval monastic architecture. Their goal was to recover and plot accurately the full ground plan of the monastery, part of an ambitious scheme to collect and distinguish the plans of monasteries of the different orders. The site was open to the public from the 1880s.

The earl's clearances revealed numerous pieces of collapsed masonry, many with architectural detailing. Regarded as superfluous to the identification of the ground plan, these stones were stacked like firewood and later removed from the ruins. Today they form an invaluable guide to the lost superstructure. Grisaille glass found in 1884 was installed in the private chapel of the earls at Sandbeck Park. Another distinguished architect, Harold Brakspear (1870–1934), continued the work and produced a phased, coloured plan of the remains in 1903.

Above: J T Micklethwaite in 1905, who worked with William St John Hope on excavations at Roche
Below: An Edwardian postcard of the 'wishing well' at Roche Abbey. The abbey site was open to the public from the 1880s and was a popular local attraction

ROCHE IN THE 20TH CENTURY

After the First World War, Roche, like many privately owned monastic sites, was placed in the guardianship of the State, which took on responsibility for its upkeep and for standards of archaeological recording. Clearance resumed in the early 1920s. 'Capability' Brown's lake was drained, the original medieval water channel was discovered and returned to use, further buried parts of the monastery to the south and west of the cloister were exposed, and limited reconstruction using recovered architectural detailing permitted a better understanding of the destroyed buildings.

This new work involved undertaking important structural stabilization of the south transept, using clearance as a public works programme for the unemployed, consolidating the walls and publishing scholarly guides. As knowledge of the site expanded after the Second World War so did the questions surrounding the former monastery. Study now turned to matters involving the graphic reconstruction of architectural features based on the recovered stonework, the interplay between the architecture and the life it was designed to serve, building sequences, wall finishes, furnishings and material culture.

This research resulted in site changes. Among the ruined abbeys of the North, Roche has always been notable for the uniform wall heights of the ruined church and monastic ranges.

Above: The north transept of the
abbey church in snow

Below: The north transept of the
abbey church, seen from across
the meadow grass

These are best explained by the radical 18th-century regularization of the medieval remains, a uniformity imposed by 'Capability' Brown that was necessary for his composition of a Picturesque landscape (which was, ironically, marked by its studied irregularity).

The painstaking exposure in the 19th and 20th centuries of the medieval remains levelled off by Brown established a new identity for the site. The remaining walls give the paradoxical impression of a monastic complex in the course of construction, rising from the ground, rather than one being demolished and its parts being carted away. Strengthening this impression was the decision in the late 1920s to employ mown grass as a verdant 'broadloom carpet' from which to view the exposed 'rooms', a domestic gardening aesthetic which confers an analytical precision. Recent replacement of some of these areas by wilder meadow grass recovers for Roche some of its ruined identity, a truer reflection of its history and the distant medieval world of which it was a part.